YOU HAVE IT ALL NOW—
YOUR LIFE IS YOURS TO DISCOVER & ENJOY

1

OTHER BOOKS BY PUBLISHER:

PSYCHOLOGY & RELIGION SHOWCASE

BEYOND THE MIND BY DADA
TOWARDS THE UNKNOWN BY DADA

ALL BOOKS CAN BE ORDERED AT:
WWW.PIONEER-COMMUNICATION.COM
FREE SHIPPING TO ALL ADDRESSES IN CANADA
AND CONTINENTAL U.S. WHEN BOOKS
ORDERED AT ABOVE WEBSITE

YOU HAVE IT ALL NOW --

YOUR LIFE IS YOURS TO DISCOVER & ENJOY

RAJ D. RAJPAL

G.C.E.(University of Cambridge, U.K.),
B.Sc.(Honors), D.A.P.R., D.M., D.C.S.,
D.P.S. (Indo-American Society),
M.B.A.(Ohio)

PIONEER COMMUNICATION

PUBLISHERS:

PIONEER COMMUNICATION CANADA

Orders for additional books can be placed directly
@ www.pioneer-communication.com

National Library of Canada Cataloguing in Publication

Rajpal Raj D., 1951-

You Have It All---Your Life is Yours to Discover and
Enjoy /Raj D. Rajpal

Includes Index

ISBN:0-9731276-5-1

This book is dedicated to all passionate people who desire an ultimate fulfillment of their Life. Such individuals want to live Life to the fullest. These blessed souls strive for total and complete enjoyment of their existence on Mother Earth. Their life is endowed with the receptivity of an open mind and innocent heart. They possess a rare affinity to new ideas, concepts and principles, which in turn help them live a 100% self- actualized Life----a Life without conflict, pain and pressure. Such special persons experience the thrill and pleasure of living Life fully at the top of the pyramid----theirs is a Life blessed with Love, Grace and Kindness.

CONTENTS

9

PREFACE

This book is dedicated to individuals who seek to live Life at the top of Maslow's pyramid of needs. Years back, a brilliant psychologist, Abraham Maslow, propounded a theory pertaining to the hierarchy of human needs. Very simply, what Maslow said was that human beings tend to strive to achieve needs in a pyramidical fashion. Imagine a pyramid, if you will, which starts broadly at the bottom and leads to a narrow top.

Now imagine the bottom of this pyramid representing your basic needs. Humans first get involved in fulfilling their basic needs for survival. For example, a human being tries to fulfill his basic needs---these are the requirement/need for food, shelter and water. Once he has secured and fulfilled these needs, he then progresses to meet with his next level of needs. The next progressively higher layer of this pyramid represents the next level of needs.

This layer is directly above the first layer of survival needs as envisioned by Dr. Maslow.

This second layer of needs can be clearly represented as safety needs, which represent an individual's requirement to live in a safe and secure environment. These needs are then followed by his need to belong and be loved.

This is then followed by an individual's need for self- esteem --- the need to achieve and gain approval and recognition by his peers in his chosen environment.

The next set of needs is cognitive needs (the need to explore Life around him).

This is then followed by aesthetic needs (appreciation of beauty).

At the highest level of this pyramid is the self-actualization need. This represents the ultimate level of living and consciousness----where a Man feels totally happy and self-realized. He lives every moment passionately and fully. He has everything he wants and needs. And every moment is perfect and complete in every way. This book is dedicated to providing a pathway, which leads towards the achievement of the goal of complete self-fulfillment and self-actualization.

Self-actualized individuals are committed to making the effort and putting in the time to do whatever it takes to live Life in a complete and continued state of Happiness.

Such unique individuals realize that Real Success in their Life has very little to do with how rich they are or how many material possessions they own.

This book tries to get you to step aside from the vastly mysterious and complex labyrinth of (your) personal relationships.

It tries to provide you an opportunity to look at your pattern of Life relationships in a detached manner.

After the book elucidates and clarifies the sources and reasons for stress and pain in one's Life, it tries to bring together this understanding in the day-to-day existence of a person--- an understanding whose application results in a more happy, centered and harmonious Life.

The book tries to piece together the various parts of the everlasting Puzzle of Life and through this process establishes some sense and sanity to one's Existence.

Through application of this newfound wisdom, it shows how one can be happy wherever one is.

This book propounds the fact that one can be happy now and stay happy tomorrow and the day after. This publication sees no conflict between happiness and the fulfillment of one's dreams and desires. This is true as long as one maintains the proper attitude and approach to Life.

Do take some time to read this book. This is not a storybook or a crime thriller.

This is a book, which attempts to mirror your Life. Read it often. Use this book as a springboard, in your attempt to live a fully integrated Life----a Life filled with Divine Grace and Love and Peace.

If this book helps you re-think some of your perceptions and opinions about Life---if this book helps you become wiser and more peaceful by learning new things on your own----then it has done its job of opening up your "wisdom and intuitive centers".

This "opening up" will help you be happier, more energetic and healthy and more complete as you go about your day-to-day challenges and experiences.

Life is merely a reflection of the quality and intensity of your relationships----this book tries to help you understand and improve such relationships. Through such improvement you become a wiser, more centered human being who is less dependent on what is happening outside you and more aware and accepting on what is happening deep within your Heart and Soul.

All progress and self-improvement is from the inside. Progress can only have an impact on an inside-out basis and never on an outside-in basis.

Inner wisdom and growth show up on the outside in terms of improved relationships with your chosen friends, family and significant other. The outside material world can never create or influence inner happiness.

Only with this knowledge and practice can you hope to learn, achieve and realize a new found truth to help you live more beautifully and harmoniously in this turbulent materialistic world.

MISSION STATEMENT

This book has a very simple and powerful mission. It seeks to encourage you to step out of your physical, emotional and intellectual shell. It urges you to challenge yourself to live your Life more vigorously, passionately and happily.

We, human beings, are experts at creating problems. Problems occur at all levels in every moment of our existence.

Some problems are clearly seen and noted by us----others are deeply sub-conscious in nature and their causes are therefore unknown to us.

At some point of time in our Life, perhaps in moments of extreme adversity and external circumstance change, do we experience a wake-up call. Our wake-up call may come in the form of a nagging loneliness or feeling of disconnection with our environment. Or this wake-up call may express itself through some strong bodily reaction This reaction could express itself through some form of physical disturbance.

Let us talk about stress as an example of physical maladjustment. Stress can cause elevated blood pressure resulting in a heart attack. Nature has a way of warning us (through our physical system) that something may be seriously wrong with our Life.

The physical disturbance is only a symptom of a more serious malady. Most individuals take treatment for stress through medications or psychological/psychiatric counseling.

However, the real test to alleviate pain and stress long-term lies not in the hands of the physician or psychiatrist-----it rests in your ability to discover the source of your unhappiness and pain and once found, your courage to take strong steps to alleviate the causes of this pain.

You may wonder and say to yourself, " I have very little stress or whatever stress I have I can control. I do not need to read this book. This book is for seriously sick people."

Nothing can be further from the truth.

We are all afflicted in some form or other. This affliction feeds itself into your Life stream and expresses itself through your Life relationships.

To accept the fact that you are weak somewhere is a rather humbling experience. However, this humbling experience is the only way to open up your Life to new suggestions and opportunities.

If you are an egoist and egotist who feel you have all of Life's answers, then please stop reading this book right now. I have, most unfortunately, no time or energy to show you a new Path.

If on the other hand, you truly desire to improve your Life, then read on.

If you believe that no one has a monopoly on any idea and that "pearls of wisdom" are there for the taking everywhere---if you sincerely desire to improve your Life and make it more beautiful and complete then read on.......

This book is dedicated to illuminating you and making you a more wiser, balanced and happy person. This book is committed to creating in you, the foundation of a person, who desires to live Life on top of the pyramid of needs.

Such a person lives his Life and enjoys every present moment of time energetically with heightened excitement and true fulfillment in an incredibly wonderful and natural world.

May this book be a simple but powerful guide to improve the quality of your relationships and give you the health, wealth and wisdom you truly deserve (but which eludes you constantly).

An open Mind, a receptive Heart, a trusting and deep enquiry can work wonders in making your Life more complete and happy in every way.

Best wishes on this remarkable and incredible journey called Life.

CHAPTER ONE

THE ROAD AHEAD

Life is a great Challenge. As you pause and look ahead, you see a Life full of unique challenges and opportunities. When you look intently with a view to observing your Road of Life ahead, you invariably pause to reflect on your past experiences----these experiences include your past opportunities and successes and also your past failures and frustrations.

You then try to subconsciously visualize where your future road could take you. This projection of your future Road Ahead is deeply influenced by your experiences of yesterday.

The Road Ahead can be a blessing and a boon or a vastly irritating and cumbersome journey. When you look ahead, you try to see some of your goals for the future; you also attempt to see the Path you have chosen for yourself, and you wonder about the relative success or failure of your future prospects and projects.

Somewhere, along this process you stop and think about all the relationships you are in and how these relationships will evolve----will these relationships survive into the future and if they do, what will be the quality and intensity of such relationships? Will these relationships bring joy and happiness and light up your Life? Or will such relationships be a real pain resulting in a vicious cycle of anger, pain and negativism? Sometimes you may think, "Why am I into these relationships? Do I really need them?"

"Is this dependence on a relationship really helping me or pulling me back in this game of Life? If I had my Life and Time again, would I engage and enter into the same relationships? Or would I do things differently?"

Very rarely do you think immediately of changing or modifying your current set of relationships. One tends to take current relationships for granted---- the tenure and duration of these relationships, however disturbing seem to provide a level of security to an individual---- a security based on the relative certainty of events crafted by such relationships.

And so, when you peer and look at the Road Ahead, there is not always a distinct opening or clear road ahead. The future is always mysterious and uncertain (however much you may try to control it or hold it in your hands today).

The Road Ahead appears sometimes as a jumbled configuration of your dreams and desires---these dreams and desires in turn are influenced by your actual day-to-day Life results, created as a direct consequence of your work and application of Life energy today.

The Road Ahead therefore represents a composite reaction to all the dreams and desires you possess for the future, influenced by current Life results.

Stop for a moment and ask yourself this question:

"How do you see your very own special Road Ahead? Is it clear and beautiful? Or is your vision of such road blurred and incomprehensible? Irrespective of how clear or blurred your image of your Road Ahead is, can you accept this vision easily?

Are you prepared to accept whatever result Life throws out your way in the future? Or do you go "bonkers" not knowing where you will be tomorrow? The Road Ahead is really only one aspect of your impression and master plan for the future. Equally important is your attitude to such Road Ahead. Can you humbly accept the fortunes of tomorrow as expressed by the Road Ahead and take it calmly in your stride? Can your Personal Happiness be uninfluenced by the results of tomorrow?

The Road Ahead can be beautiful or painful. It all depends on your approach and attitude and most importantly on your Life Values as you weather Life's storms.

Will you weather these storms happily and peacefully or will you react to these storms with anxiety and stress? You really do have a choice through application of the proper attitude and approach to the Future.

Is the foundation of your personal value system strong enough to allow you to face and accept with total happiness and abandon the results of tomorrow?

Or are you brainwashed by your culture to try to control not only your chosen Life activities but also the results, which flow from application of your Life energy in such activities?

Are you constantly trying to control your relationships, your material wealth and your Life that you sometimes do not know how to savor and enjoy this moment?

This moment is really the only thing promised to you by Existence. Can you enjoy this moment completely, counting your blessings for all His Gifts to you?

Or are you totally blind to the moment as you pursue future dreams, plans and goals?

This chapter wants to encourage and motivate you to think about your special journey ahead----it wants you to sit quietly and ponder about the pictures, sensations, feelings and processes, which are activated when you close your eyes and look at your own very special Road Ahead.

Can you in this instant second, picture where you will be five, ten or twenty years from now?

On the other hand, if you cannot clearly picture your future (and this is fine, too) ---can you be totally Happy both with whatever point you are at now and with whatever point you may be at five, ten or twenty years forward?

Needless to say, it is not always the people who are adept at planning and achieving their goals, who are the happiest and most successful in their Life. Success is a unique and highly misunderstood phenomenon.

Success really arrives through the feeling of being Happy in whatever state you are in now.

Success also involves an open invitation to happiness to touch your Life tomorrow irrespective of what state you may be in tomorrow, (financially, emotionally, physically and spiritually).

Success is not arriving anywhere----it is knowing who you are, being strengthened by your foundation of Life values and having a positive loving attitude to everyone. Success is building and strengthening the foundation of your relationships.

The Road Ahead is the first part of this journey we undertake together.

Look ahead and see what this Road means to you. Everyone's experience will throw out a different image of this Road Ahead. Are you happy with your image and expectation of this Road Ahead?

Is the picture you see really where you'd like to be five, ten or twenty years from now? Or does this picture belong to someone else. Or is this picture one, which is forced upon you by other external influences?

If you cannot see any clear picture of the Road Ahead, then are you happy with this empty, unfulfilled, non-materialized vision?

Look at your Road Ahead as you attempt to build a bigger, total, integrated Life picture of how you can fulfill your happiness and justify your Destiny.

Our Destiny is to be happy and live every moment harmoniously and lovingly with a great deal of passion and energy.

CHAPTER TWO

WHERE YOU ARE NOW

This moment is probably the most "significant" point of Time in our Life. But through our cultural, educational and environmental influences, we tend to diminish the value of TODAY as we strive towards numerous goals and objectives into the future.

The present has, in many ways become meaningless. We usually live in our past or get pre-occupied with our tomorrow's as we work to achieve results into the future.

The present appears to be only a means to an end--- a bridge used to achieve whatever we desire in the future.

What a foolish waste of our Energy? The present is all that is promised to us. The past is dead and gone and the future is not known. This present moment and our capacity and ability to appreciate and enjoy it completely represents the true barometer of our happiness and self-actualization.

If you can close your eyes right now and get in touch with your Life---if you feel Happy and exalted in the awareness and perception that you are totally happy, blessed and complete, then you have everything you need. You need not get richer or sexier or have a bigger home or car. You have it all ---your Life is yours to discover and enjoy right now and for ever into the future, ad infinitum.

Since this is not how most people feel, let us get back to building the bigger picture of the Road Ahead.

Let us try to understand why it is so difficult to feel completely fulfilled at this moment.

Let us look at how normal people view themselves in real Life and in real Time. A normal person when asked to respond to a question, " Where are you Now?", automatically looks at all his Life results today as reflected by the culmination of all his relationship results in the past. Let me expand this concept. You live in America or Canada. You were brought up in a certain family or religious environment.

You created or genetically inherited certain desires and hopes as you grew up.

Some of your dreams came true and some dreams did not come to fruition. As you grew and entered into relationships, some relationships were satisfying and some were not. You looked at where you are today as a sum total (evaluation) of all your Life experiences and relationships. You then applied a judgment or value factor to these successes or failures.

Where one person had some level of contentment and happiness with a life relationship score of 9/10, another person could go "bonkers" and get depressed at this score.

Let us assume you developed this scoring system by giving yourself one point for every satisfying result in the past and you had ten major life experiences, each of which was assigned a score of 1 for being satisfying and a score of 0 for being non-satisfying).

Where you see yourself today is critical in your understanding of where you will go tomorrow.

Also important in your vision of tomorrow is a clear understanding and awareness of the nature of your evaluation system.

Composition of this evaluation system and your understanding of how you are applying this system in judging your past results will help you understand what makes you happy or sad today.

Happiness releases adrenaline and positive hope for tomorrow. Sadness creates depression and a negative energy field as you move into the realm of tomorrow.

So sadness or happiness can make a critical impact on your Life tomorrow. And the most overlooked fact is that you and you alone are responsible for inviting happiness or sadness in your Life. Either you work consistently to create an inner environment and strong value system, which attracts happiness into your Life or by default, sadness, will undeniably enter your Life.

An important test of your current physical, emotional, intellectual and spiritual health is the response to this important question:

"WHERE ARE YOU NOW?"

Ask yourself this question without direction or purpose. Just feel how you feel when you respond to this question. Do you feel happy with your results in today's time?

Or do you feel unhappy with the results? Or do you feel certain results are good while others are not?

It is most critical when you evaluate your Life results that you be aware of what judgmental and evaluation system you are using. Are your perceptions of your progress clouded by your spouse's view? Your parents view? Your friend's view?

Or are they clouded by a cultural or peer group view? Are you happy with the evaluation system you are using now?

What thoughts, ideas and feelings come up when you answer this question,

" WHERE AM I TODAY?"

Do spend as much time as you like on this question. Write down your responses to this question. Analyze your answers frequently.

The answer or lack of concrete answer will throw up your established psychological value system, the knowledge of your evaluation system and the nature and diversity of goals sought by you in the past.

Through this deep process of enquiry, you must honestly ask yourself the following questions:

1. Am I happy with my evaluation system for my results?

2. Are these goals I formulated and fought for in the past really mine?

   Or am I trying to fulfill someone else's standards and

dreams through my past goals?

3. What is my psychological value system? What do I really believe in? Do I have a strong core of moral or other fundamental values, which guide me through my Life?

4. If I were to change any part of my psychological value system or modify some of my goals, would I be happier now?

5. Am I denying myself any happiness by being too hard on myself?

6. Is there a simpler way of achieving my dreams and goals with less stress or pain?

Where you see yourself Now (when you look at the Road Ahead) creates a certain impact and trend in your process of attaining and maintaining happiness.

Let us now proceed to the next part of the puzzle----where you want to be tomorrow. This is the subject matter of Chapter 3 of this book.

CHAPTER 3

WHERE YOU WANT TO BE
TOMORROW

Desire forms the wellspring of all positive movement   forward. And desire   steadily   and   strongly influences the course and results of one's future actions.

As you look at the Road Ahead and survey where you are today, looking into the future can be real fun if you have a strong , passionate urge to get whatever you want and choose in your Life.

Unfortunately, this matter of Desire is really hard to understand and even more harder to implement in your plans for the future. Invariably, your past results as reflected in how you feel about where you are today, influence the intensity and direction of your desires pertaining to where you want to be tomorrow. A lot of individuals negate or underestimate the true value of strong desire.

In several instances, if an individual wanted something intensely in the past and could not get it, this past result could cause a lack of confidence and a reduced level of desire. This is particularly true if this individual tries to achieve a failed dream of the past, into the future.

It is critical to understand the strong effect of positive energy flowing from a well-nurtured desire---and how such strong energy can dominate (to fruition) your direction for tomorrow.

In the Western world, there is a preponderance and an unreasonable emphasis placed on planning and implementing Life and Business strategies.

The role of desire is relegated to a somewhat unnecessary function.

It is important for an individual to give separate and special emphasis to allowing Desire to open up a productive channel to make great things happen in the future.

Ask yourself what it is that you really want in the future. Suspend all judgment and fear when you let your mind and heart ponder on what would really make you happy in your relationships and Life results in the future. It is only after you give yourself permission to want without judgment and comparison that you really have a good shot at understanding your wellspring of motivation.

Channeling your emotional energy in the direction of your dreams will help you get what you really want in the future.

Let your mind float freely----let your heart be casual and playful as you dream about:

1. Your ideal relationships in the future.

2. Your ideal vocation or avocation.

3. Your results in situations, which would make you most happy.

Once permission is given to your heart to justify and express its innermost needs and wants, plotting and creating your perfect emotional future becomes easier.

Awareness and acceptance of this emotional power will unleash a dynamic and dynamite source of energy, which will help you get whatever you feel you want and need in the future.

CHAPTER 4

WHERE YOU THINK YOU SHOULD
BE TOMORROW

As you ponder into the future, your Mind, through your thought processes, starts influencing your concept of where you want to be tomorrow. It is really important to distinguish between feelings and wants as described in Chapter 3 and intellectual and analytical contemplation as presented and explained through this chapter.

Depending on your genetic composition, your natural intellectual abilities and your environment and cultural conditionings, you may have a greater or lesser disposition to rationalizing your vision of the future. There is no right or wrong way to look into the future. Every human being is unique and therefore has his special way of projecting himself and his relationships into the future. The critical part in successful future intellectual projection is the balance achieved between emotions and intellect in one's achievement of a future vision.

A very strong intellect can cause confusion and conflict in achieving what one sees as good for one's future. An extremely strong emotional pull can also cause a similar effect. What is required is a smooth and happy balance between the mind and heart. This is easier said than done.

When you look at the Road Ahead, you may choose to balance your emotional with your intellectual aspirations to create a smooth Life result in getting what you see as important for your tomorrow.

Awareness of the strength and personal disposition of an individual emotionally or intellectually can help smooth out any rough edges.

When one asks oneself, "Where do you think you should be tomorrow?" and compares the answers with the question, "Where do you want to be tomorrow?" one often finds a conflict in the intellectual and emotional responses to this question. The intellectual response could be quite different from the emotional response. This conflict then reflects itself in the quality of your future results.

It is important to view any discrepancies between where you want to be tomorrow (emotional motivation) and where you think you should be tomorrow (intellectual motivation), Learning to bridge these differences and creating a uniform integrated front for your future is essential to making your Life more meaningful and productive in the future.

CHAPTER 5

WHERE YOU OUGHT TO BE
TOMORROW

Sometimes one experiences a nagging question, which has no easy or straightforward answer. This nagging and unanswerable question is, " Where ought I to be tomorrow?" The "ought issue" surrounding this question normally represents a third party point of view. Let me explain.

Ever since times immemorial, we have been brainwashed by others into believing what is best for our Life. This influence could come from a variety of sources. There is constantly a comparison between the way our Life is and what our Life should be as judged by other people's and/or Society's standards. Sometimes these "other people", who try to impose their standards on us, are the very ones who are most near and dear to us.

When you look at the Road Ahead and contemplate which direction you want to move in tomorrow, there is this constant interference between what you want, what you think you need and where you feel you ought to be tomorrow.

The "ought to be tomorrow syndrome" creates a tremendous guilt in an individual---particularly if the individual's goals do not correspond with societal or cultural goals imposed on him environmentally.

Several individuals are not even aware of the massive influence other people's agenda have on their own personal lives.

Ask yourself these questions:

Looking at tomorrow, do you :

1. Feel guilty about certain things you did or did not do in the past?

2. Feel you must re-align your goals and expectations and vision to make other's happy?

3. Feel you need to win the confidence and approval of friends and society, which has resulted in making choices today you are not happy with?

4. Feel you are moving in a certain direction but are not happy going there? You have only moved in this direction for someone else's reason and cannot find the courage and strength to change course mid-stream.

When looking at the Road Ahead one must discount and eliminate any actions, decisions and movements done to please others. Such movements do not represent your true feelings and thoughts on where you want to go tomorrow.

Awareness of the " ought to syndrome" accompanied with the courage and conviction to chart your Life direction based on your true needs and wishes, will help you live a more centered and happy Life.

CHAPTER 6

YOUR ENVIRONMENT AND ITS CHALLENGES—THE OBSTACLES IN YOUR PATH

The environment plays a crucial role in the nourishment, growth and current composition of your personality. Most individuals do not realize that they carry around in their personality a figment/impression of their past and current environmental conditioning.

And this impression whether conscious or subconscious, has the capacity to make a vital difference between happiness and misery in your Life.

All environmental influences feed into the conscious and/or sub- conscious make up of your personality. The environment around us is constantly changing and therefore the environmental influence is constantly changing and acting upon our psyche.

Environmental influences may be
divided into the following three
categories:

1. PAST ENVIRONMENTAL
   INFLUENCES
   These influences start from
   birth. Depending on where
   you were born in the world
   and how you were influenced
   by the personality and value
   system of your parents, you
   started constituting
   psychologically in a specific,
   unique fashion.
   Several strong influences in

the first six to eight years of your Life subtly created a mould and influenced your personality. As you grew through puberty and maturity, these influences hid in sub-conscious levels of your Mind.

One of the great challenges facing a human being is the ability to tap into this mysterious sub – conscious aspect of your mind----becoming aware in the process of what such hidden influences are--- once this understanding is complete, one can proceed to understand how such influences effect not only one's current personality but also shape one's reactions to Life challenging situations in the present and future.

2. CURRENT
ENVIRONMENTAL
INFLUENCES

These influences play an immediate and dynamic role in your perception of your Life around you now. Your relationships with your spouse or significant other, your relationships at work and your relationships with your physical environment and your friends and immediate social surrounding play a great role in your perception of Life around you.

These environmental forces are too numerous to mention. However, each environmental force exerts a demand on your energy and through the maze of demands, you decide, sometimes quite subconsciously as to which direction your Life will take. Again, a complete detached awareness of every environmental force around you and its current impact on you would help tremendously in determining which direction you are moving in and help you determine what obstacles may lie ahead.

3. FUTURE ENVIRONMENTAL INFLUENCES

These influences are in the unknown and mysterious future realm. There is no way of knowing what results you will achieve tomorrow, since future results are deciphered through an unknown Space in future Time. When your Energy and Effort collides in Time with future Space, the results can be quite uncertain and unpredictable.

Here it is critical that one does not show a high level of anxiety in trying to time and control every future result. There is also the constant noise of Society and Culture, which extols winners and denies losers any recognition of their effort. This invariably creates more pressure on part of an individual to control or assure certain pre-determined results in the future.

Your environmental challenges represent all the factors in the external and internal environment, which influence your ability to get what you want.

More importantly, the environmental forces impacting on your Life Path tend to create either a high level of Pain or a great level of Happiness and Contentment, depending on whether you are winning and getting what you want or missing your targets miserably.

A way of going above and beyond this environmental effect of Pain or Happiness is your ability to go beyond this Game of Life; becoming and staying happy at whatever point you are in today and at whatever point you reach tomorrow.

Most of us find this extremely hard to do, because we get habituated in punishing ourselves through the medium of pain, anguish, guilt and denial. This punishment is more apparent when we do not appear to get what we want. On the other hand, we are exalted and excited if we keep winning constantly and consistently.

Let us talk more about internal environmental factors. The real environment is not really outside you. It is primarily inside you. Let me explain. You are responsible for crafting ideal strategies for your Life. You are also responsible for your happiness. Your inner sanctum, your inner space controls all results on the outside. It is crucial to be aware of all the components of your personality. How much time have you spent with yourself lately? This does not include time playing hockey or baseball or in attention to your idiot box (TV set).

What I mean is quality meditative time trying to understand yourself thoroughly, including an understanding of your needs, wants and motivations.

The inner environment must be understood thoroughly and then this understanding will help create strength in getting what you want on the outside.

The inner strength will give you the courage and patience to wait till things happen your way and allow you not to quit mid-stream (before your dreams of happiness and success are realized).

The external environment is comprises the influence of all things happening outside you. This could include things happening in your job or business, things happening in your relationships with your loved ones or with your adversaries.

The inner environment on the other hand has a connection with all the reactions to the external environment. Ordinarily, the inner environment is assumed to be an offshoot of your external environment. In fact, it is the other way around.

Your inner values, your inner confidence level, your energy level and inner strength determine the quality and impact of the external environment on your Life. A strong inner environment creates a more stable, reliable and happy reaction to external environmental influences and creates the right atmosphere to succeed in a spirit of love and harmony.

The understanding and awareness of your inner sanctum will help provide an easy path for you as you work through any negatives in the external environment, giving you courage to hold on till you get what you want.

As you move through your Life, you will face obstacles. An obstacle is any situation or person, which prevents you from getting what you want in Real Time.

How you face such an obstacle is crucial in your ability to win eloquently or lose miserably in achieving any of your Life goals. How do you face up to an obstacle?

90

Do you immediately acquire a confrontational attitude when some person comes in the way of your happiness or do you try to achieve what you want by enlisting the support of someone even if that someone appears dark and ominous today?

Do you face Life confidently or with a negative energy filled with frustration and stress?

Do you believe that you can work with and through people to get what you want, irrespective of how tough or hard they may be on you?

Do you pray and ask the Almighty to give you the strength to attract what you want without hurting or destroying anyone? Your attitude is critical and crucial factor influencing your ability to attract success and happiness in your Life.

To sum up this chapter, one needs to have an accepting mind and open heart to all problems ahead.

One needs to re-translate a problem as a challenge and opportunity to improve oneself.

One needs to accept the fact that there will be obstacles in the external environment. This is merely a fact of Life.

One must be supremely aware of one's inner environment and of one's inner conditioning and wants and needs. Through this understanding and acceptance one must build a strong inner foundation, which allows you to weather the storms and obstacles on the outside.

You have one of two choices:

Either sulk or get stressed out trying to overcome external obstacles in your path to success & inner fulfillment.

Or you can be happy and innocent like a child, who plays with every problem, translating such problem into a challenge and learning to find a way out of any situation in order to fulfill a desired objective.

A problem becomes a challenge, an obstacle becomes a game, which must be won by a child ---- a setback becomes another challenge to overcome.

Why not be a child once more and learn to win and stay on top of everything all the time? And why not be happy through this journey of Life?

Happiness is in the Present----the happier you are today, the more successful you will be in getting what you want tomorrow.

The latter choice is the only worthwhile choice in your quest for peace, fulfillment and success.

CHAPTER 7

OVERCOMING OBSTACLES ON YOUR PATHWAY TO SUCCESS

Let us get into the subject area of methods of overcoming obstacles you may encounter on your pathway to success.

An obstacle is anything you perceive as getting in the way of your happiness today and in the realization of your dream for tomorrow.

It is really important to dream, because without dreams there can be no real progress or change in the future.

However, Happiness today and Happiness tomorrow is far more important than just making a dream come true or fulfilling a fancy wish. If you are unhappy in spite of all your dreams being fulfilled, then what is the value of your dreams????

There was an interesting but incredibly foolish story I was brainwashed with in sales school (this happened in the early '70s).

In this sales school an instructor pointed out a novel definition of commercial success. The instructor defined Success as. " the worthwhile realization of a pre-determined goal".

And once an individual achieved this goal, he was called upon to create a new goal and then direct his energy to achieve this next.-------if an individual did not engage in this constant process of goal-setting and goal fulfillment he was not considered successful. And this cycle kept going on and on with no end in sight.

What an incredibly idiotic concept as far as the application of this definition of success to the presence of personal happiness!!!

Success is the complete opposite of this relentless process of setting goals and achieving them in mechanical sequence. Success, in fact, is not arriving anywhere. Success can be found and discovered when it has a capacity to create the spark of happiness in an individual. Happiness is the ultimate elixir of Life. But Happiness cannot be hurried or created on demand.

Happiness is the by-product of a great deal of awareness and intelligence deep within us. Success is synonymous with Happiness.

Let us now talk a little about something you really want or need in your Life today. You have dedicated hours and hours of effort working towards this end----however, the result you want is eluding you. For some strange reason, some obstacle or another presents itself in the external environment. You seem to be hitting your head hard against the wall but no result is immediately forthcoming. How do you overcome the obstacles in your way?

For one thing, do not fight with the obstacle. Let it be there. Accept its presence for the time being.

Keep applying your energy in your chosen direction. Focus more on your inner strengths and value system.

Believe totally and perfectly that you will get what you want not only because you have put in the effort but also because you truly deserve the result. Distract your consciousness from the obstacle. Shift your attention and energy to the task at hand.

You must believe that you can get anything you want and Success will be yours.

Let us look at how you can positively change your inner environment to get what you want. Your inner environment is the true environment you must face and understand. Meditation results in a quick and keen understanding of your inner environment. Meditation is the quickest and most effective way of:

    a) Harnessing your Inner Energy

    b) Understanding your inner environment's functioning.

Sit in a quiet place with no distractions. Try to get a total view of your goal and desire. See clearly what your obstacles are. Accept these obstacles as a temporary sojourn for you. Go deep into yourself to see how you are reacting from an inner point of view to the obstacle. Are you getting stressed out or trying to escape from the task at hand? If you see that, then stay with that feeling. Don't fight it. Slowly, but surely as you meditate intensively, you will find a natural strength and energy which will assist you in overcoming the obstacles ahead.

Go about your work the next day with renewed vigor and confidence and positivism and success will be yours. However, work with Happiness today. Accept your Happiness as unconditional. Your Happiness has nothing to do with whether you achieve your goal or not. And your quality of Happiness and Energy has nothing to do with whether you achieve your goal tomorrow or after five years. Your happiness is unconditional. Your energy is complete today.

With this approach and attitude, you will almost always get what you want and need.

Confidence, happiness and harmony in all your actions will mysteriously remove all your obstacles and get you what you want.

This is true as long as you believe you deserve the very best in your Life and that obstacles are only temporary tests to make you a better, brighter and more composed human being tomorrow.

CHAPTER 8

AND WHAT IS SUCCESS???

We have spent the first seven chapters together discussing numerous issues.

We first visualized our own Personal Road Ahead; we then looked at where we were today. We then proceeded to look at what we wanted in our lives tomorrow. We then shifted our observation to what we thought we might like tomorrow.

We then studied the "ought to syndrome"---how we viewed what others perceived we should have in our Life.

We then looked at how there were inherent conflicts between what we wanted tomorrow and what we thought was important for us tomorrow and what we thought we ought to have tomorrow. The author then tried to urge an individual to create some balance between his emotions and intellect and disregard what others might want for him.

Then the discussion moved on to one's inner and external environment and the importance of focusing on one's inner environment. We looked at how an understanding of your inner environment was valuable in allowing you to easily overcome Life obstacles------ such obstacles invariably frustrated the achievement of an individual's goal.

We then discussed obstacles in the way of a person's success and presented some novel ways to overcome such obstacles.

However, along this marvelous journey called Life, the author forgot to mention the definition of success or what we were really after.

So, to round out our discussion and create some perspective to our presentation, let us dive into the subject of success. What is Success? Is there something, which constitutes your success? And something else, which constitutes my success as opposed to yours? Are visions of success different?

Or are different visions of future deeply connected to each other even though one person's definition of success may differ from another person's definition?

I see only one definition of success:

"SUCCESS S A HAPPY, HEIGHTENED STATE OF CONSCIOUSNESS FULL OF ENERGY, PASSION AND LOVE. SUCCESS IS A NEVER ENDING EXPRESSION OF LOVE, HARMONY AND GOODNESS IN A PERSON.

SUCCESS IS THE POSSESSION AND MAINTENANCE OF GOOD QUALITY RELATIONSHIPS WITH FAMILY, FRIENDS, NATURE, IDEAS AND PROPERTY."

Success is not being very rich or having a lot of toys or owning a lot of material things. Success is being happy today with whatever you have and having the confidence that you will be fulfilled wherever Life takes you tomorrow. Success is giving yourself the permission to be unconditionally happy now and in the future.

However, Society has created a different definition of success and we most unfortunately allow ourselves to be controlled and influenced by their definition of success.

In the world, material success is not guaranteed to anyone all the time.

However, we make it our Life's goal to achieve material success (as defined by our society and culture) all the time and maintain it ad infinitum in the future. Success in Society is defined as getting whatever you choose to desire, usually accompanied with great external material success.

In the world, we have individuals with different levels of ability and knowledge and luck and this creates a massive difference in success results for different individuals.

Society is adept at creating evaluation standards for successful and unsuccessful people.

And we all try to emulate the world image of success and get frustrated if we are considered as failures in any endeavor.

There is no doubt that we need certain things as a minimum. A decent house, a reasonably nice car, a loving home and family and good relationships with friends and some security for our old age are most important. But once you reach these goals, where do you go next? Do you invest your energy and time in acquiring an even bigger house, an even bigger car or maybe a sexier partner? Where does this end?

Is this the way of our Life? Is this the way of Happiness and Harmony? And if it is, how can we ever expect to be happy----we are constantly searching, never fulfilled, and never satisfied.

So when we look at the issue of success we must view it very privately in terms of what we have today and what we really need.

We must really question what we really want. Are we going to go the North American way of bigger cars, bigger homes, more money, more sex, more intellectual stimulation, more alcohol or can we truly simplify our Lives?

If we can start thinking of simplifying our Lives, we can start a process of attracting happiness------...otherwise happiness will merely become a concept----something we dream and fantasize about but never something we can really touch and enjoy and savor in our Life. Being happy and thinking about achieving happiness are two totally different things.

If we can agree on a universal definition of success, then we know that unconditional acceptance of our state now and an acceptance in the future of our Personal Life results will guarantee us a longer and more abiding form of happiness.

This does not mean that one must not aspire to have a better life; it just means that there is a refusal to allow your happiness to be impacted by the fact that you have or have not achieved certain Life results today and/or tomorrow.

Success operates both at an inner level and on an outer level. Outer level success is obtaining by acquiring and maintaining some of the basic requirements in life like a nice house, a reasonable car, a happy home, good friends and a reasonably free and amiable environment in a free democratic country. Once we have this, is it possible to go into the understanding of Inner success?

Inner success is being passionate about Life and Nature. Inner success is being compassionate and loving and caring for your neighbor the way you would for your family. Inner success is trying to help others weaker and less privileged than you. Inner success is never hurting someone else to get up your ladder of external success.

Inner success means being empathic and loving to all human beings and creatures. Inner success most importantly, is understanding yourself and connecting with the Great Power around us and living a happy simple life.

So if one only judges happiness by getting whatever one wants and wishes, then one is setting oneself up for a life of misery and delusion. Happiness is not just getting anything you want impulsively.

What you want must have some purpose and connection with Life and (helping)Humanity---otherwise it is a selfish, self-centered goal, which will never result in long term happiness and prosperity.

Most of us are happy trying to get whatever we want, thinking that what we want will keep us happy and fulfill our lives.

Happiness, Harmony and Integration in Life cannot be ordered on demand. These are the toughest things to experience and maintain. In fact, they happen by default.

They are the by-product of a life of simplicity, humility and heightened self-awareness.

Where one chooses to go is one's own choice. However, the next time you have achieved something, ask yourself the following questions:

1.   Have I truly helped someone else in the process of my work and expression?

2.   Have I given more than I have gained by a certain activity?

3.   Have I actively shared some of the fruits of my success with others less fortunate and talented than me?

4.   Have I tried to improve the quality of my relationships with my loved ones and with my environment or is success only a matter of acquisition of more dollars and toys?

TRUE SUCCESS is a smile on your face all the time.

TRUE SUCCESS is an ever-present twinkle in your eye.

TRUE SUCCESS is giving more than taking.

TRUE SUCCESS is an ever-shining happy glow around you.

So, what do you want? More material things? More love? More happiness?

I guess you can craft any possible definition of the meaning and significance of Success in your Life. However, before you rush in setting and crystallizing this definition in your Mind, try to look at success from several angles. .Do look at success from a multi-dimensional perspective.

Try to apply new definitions of success and see if you are coming closer to living a truly happy and loving life by applying a specific definition.

This is your Life. Make it as Happy and Alive as you can.

Do not allow misconceived definitions of Success come in the way of your God given right to be truly happy.

Life is meant to attract Happiness and Love into your consciousness----without happiness and love, Life has no meaning at all. This chapter is designed to get you to stretch your imagination and consciousness to help you live a more fuller, complete and happier life, on your own terms.

CHAPTER 9

THE ILLUSION OF A DESTINATION

We seem to be brainwashed into wanting to reach some place all the time. And we spend countless hours of time, energy and effort in trying to reach some destination point in our Life. We craft numerous plans to achieve such destination points. We feel that once we reach this point, our Life destination is at least temporarily fulfilled.

And then we try to reach for another destination goal and then we again reach this point. And we set another goal. And sometimes we set numerous goals simultaneously, which we strive to achieve.

And this is the never-ending cycle of business, personal and religious Life--- a series of destination goals, which need to be reached to fulfill the cycle of our Life.

Although in an external business and work sense, it may be imperative to fulfill the goals of your employer or business-----is there really any intrinsic, deeper and significant happiness in just hitting and reaching goals on the external Life front?

When we look at truly understanding ourselves in relationship to others, and in relationship to nature, ideas and possessions, is there any lasting and abiding effect of either picking a destination or arriving at it?

Or is true Success knowing that Life is far more significant and vital than either setting or reaching a destination goal? Society through its competitive mechanisms has made the destination not only important for an individual aspiring to external success----but also added a new element to the definition of success: the speed with which you reach this destination is more critical (than just reaching the destination) in measuring the economic and outward success of a citizen.

People who hit the ball furthest, who run the fastest, are the special ones who are revered and showered with incredible wealth and social recognition. These are the model citizens of the world as exposed and propounded by the media and our peer groups.

But is emulating the fastest and externally smartest the way to genuine and true happiness?

When you really look at your Life, is it possible to be happy where you are today without comparing your results with your neighbor or any other competitor?

You have it all now ----your Life is yours to truly discover and relish from moment to moment. However, if you are constantly looking over your shoulder endlessly to determine who is running faster than you or who is running slower than you but is about to overtake you in the competitive game of Life, do you have any hope or chance of being happy either today or tomorrow?

It is impossible to be happy now or ever in the future if all your understanding of Life is limited to external competitive activity which either labels you as a winner or loser.

You can win in Life by stopping the comparisons----you can have it all now by throwing out and discarding all the foolish and stupid competitive values of Society.

This does not mean that you stop exerting effort nor does it mean that you stop trying to be the very best you can be in whatever you do. It just means you shift your attitude to one of working non-competitively. It means you have the confidence that you can do a job or business superlatively by competing with yourself and not with your neighbor.

Unless you operate with this newfound vision, which incorporates a non-competitive attitude, all your destination goals will be illusory and counter-productive to a happy, healthy and prosperous Life.

SO YOU HAVE REACHED YOUR DESTINATION???

When reaching a destination becomes the most important purpose in your Life, you feel exalted and happy on getting to your predetermined destination goal in the right amount of time.

131

You have spent weeks, months or years in reaching your goal. You have had to face numerous obstacles to reach this important point of completion. You have probably spent several sleepless nights planning your ultimate victory and now you have it. Suddenly all the pain and discomfort in achieving this end point are forgotten. You are finally victorious. You are happy and self-indulgent now. You are now waiting to get the golden reward for your hard work. At this critical point you seem happy and self-fulfilled. Life at this point is beautiful.

You will be rewarded by a big bonus check and a job promotion. You start imagining how you will spend this extra money----you may probably move to a bigger home or buy a bigger, more fancy car. And you are so happy!!!!

Is this true happiness? Or is this happiness a fleeting session? Is your true Life success fulfilled when you meet and exceed a particular business goal?

Or is it that this fleeting success today will be replaced with an anxiety and pressure to reach an even higher business goal established by your business partners or corporation tomorrow?

What lesson can you learn if you are very good at what you do and reach your destination goals easily and effectively? The lesson to be learnt is that one part of your Life is moving reasonably well --- now you have the time and energy to focus on other vital parts of your Life.

Important issues like enhancing the quality of your relationships, spending more time with loved ones and friends and giving back some of your success to your community through service, become important considerations now.

AT WHAT PRICE HAVE YOU REACHED YOUR DESTINATION?

When one exerts effort, time and money in achieving a certain destination goal, does one pay particular attention to what price one pays for achieving that goal?

135

Price to achieve a destination goal can be viewed through two perspectives:

Firstly, the exact and actual quantum of energy and effort exerted to achieve a particular goal.

Secondly, the price to reach your destination can be viewed in terms of the cost of reaching that goal. Simply, this is the opportunity cost----where else could you have exerted the same amount of effort and energy to achieve another worthwhile goal or Life result?

AND WHERE DO YOU GO FROM HERE?

So, you have either reached or failed in reaching a particular destination goal,

If you have reached your destination goal, where do you go from here?

Is happiness in setting and exceeding an even bigger goal? Or if you have not reached your goal, is there a purpose in continually trying to achieve this unrealized and unfulfilled goal? Or is happiness in abandoning the process of reaching that goal?

These are questions every knowledgeable person must ask himself with a view of developing a good Life strategy.

OUTER SUCCESS IS NOT A DESTINATION—IT IS A PROCESS

Outer success is normally measured by what you need as a human being to live comfortably in your surroundings. All economic and material gain takes the application of your talent in a specialized field.

It also involves hitting certain pre-determined goals set by your corporation, employer or business partners.

Unless you decide to live in a cave and survive on (hunted) fresh fruits and oxygen you need to work in an organized social and business set up. To earn enough to buy/carry a house, own a car, live a comfortable life you need a constant flow of capital. This capital is normally earned in the form of income, generated through a job, profession or business.

Income is consistently earned if you can fulfill someone else's goals (if you work for someone else) or by satisfying your customer's needs, if you have your own business.

Outer success is a starting point for inner success. There can be no long-term inner success if some of your basic needs are not consistently met.

I have not seen one happy person who is hungry or has no roof over his head.

With respect to external success, certain requirements are paramount.

140

One has to create and maintain an ability to be employable to earn consistent income. However, this is only a starting point. The real success and happiness lies beyond this plane of existence. However, outer success too, is not a destination but a process. The process refers to the things one must do to achieve certain goals in the external world like earning enough income to keep his home, to have good meals and to do all the things to protect a chosen lifestyle.

However, the attitude with which you proceed in this outer realm is critical.

Outer success is not one particular destination, which defines the end of effort and energy application. It is a constant, shifting process, where one keeps adjusting and adapting to his environment to stay employable.

If one views outer success as a constant process of adjustment and change to adapt and adjust to the business world, which feeds him, then one has a more healthy attitude to his chosen vocation/avocation.

CHAPTER 10

COMBINING OUTER SUCCESS
WITH INNER SUCCESS

The last chapter talked about how important it was for every person to reach such external goals as required to assure a certain level of external success. However, the real challenge of happiness was to go beyond the process of reaching his potential for external success. How would such an individual make a shift from external to inner success?

I guess everything would start from a healthy self-examination of one's personality make-up and an understanding of one's needs, wants and desires. In this process of analysis, one would have to make a subjective decision of the value of a pre-established need, want and desire. Specifically, what would one have to do in terms of application of time, effort and energy to achieve all his various dreams and desires? Would there be a point where one could cut off certain desires or dreams to live a happier and simpler Life?

Inner success has very little to do with external success.

Inner success means being happy and balanced in your inner space.

Inner success means acquiring a good balance between your mental and emotional health.

Inner success means having a healthy constitution and respecting and adequately nourishing your body.

Inner success means not taking to heart any difficulties you may have in achieving your external goals, but staying happy unconditionally now and in the future.

It means having the capacity and faith in allowing yourself only happiness and gratitude in every aspect and moment in your Life.

Inner success is not a process but an end result, a by-product of right living, thinking and action.

Outer success can be viewed as an external frame within which inner success breeds and flourishes.

If one truly desires peace, harmony and love in one's Life, one must strive to simplify one's Life. One must truly be able to enjoy the simple and beautiful things in Nature and be truly meditative.

146

Inner success is the true challenge of Life----external success is only the first step to opening up the Time and Space for a person to pursue more significant and meaningful Life goals.

If one views inner success as the ultimate goal of Life, then one does not take external success too seriously-----external success is only a means and not an end in creating peace and harmony in one's Life.

If you truly desire to enjoy Life today by understanding and accepting the truth that you have everything you need today to be happy----then you have the capacity to truly discover your Life today.

Inner success means being happy and contented now and all the time. Inner success is a happiness you will feel with the right understanding and awareness of Life and of all your relationships around you. Inner success is not something, which can be forced down your consciousness.

It is definitely not a "made to order" phenomenon. It is, on the contrary, something created through simplicity and right thinking, feeling and action.

CHAPTER 11

THE STRUGGLE TO ARRIVE
INWARDLY

As we progress to reach a state of inner happiness and inner success, we unfortunately apply the same standards to this process as we do to our external Life Success. Let me explain. External success requires setting and achieving goals within well defined Time limits.

External success involves a certain level of struggle to overcome obstacles to get what you want and need in terms of goal fulfillment.

When we shift to our inner consciousness, we feel that a similar kind of struggle is also required in this inner realm. Nothing is further from the truth. Inner happiness cannot be created on demand. On the contrary, inner unhappiness can be viewed as a barometer of something going wrong in our Life now. Inner success cannot be hurried. Inner success is really not a goal. It is a benevolent happening.

It is really simple to ask yourself if you are totally happy with every aspect in your Life.

If you are not, then you are judging yourself internally as you would judge yourself externally.

Inner happiness and success does not call for the same standards of performance as external happiness. Instead, it calls for the exercise of simplicity and austerity.

An acceptance of your quality of inner happiness at whatever point you feel you are at now is a beginning.

From this point of acceptance, one must, through awareness and inner observation be aware of any potential conflicts and pain which might distract an individual and move him along a path of denial and guilt and pain. Through awareness one can deflect one's inner negativism into inner positivism. One can work through awareness at staying happy now and refusing to be unhappy tomorrow because of any Life result, which may not be suitable in the external realm. This kind of attitude calls for eternal self-watchfulness.

And a confidence that Life will always be good and kind and helpful to you. It means accepting that there are forces in work in Nature and Life which are not always under your control and which need not be under our control all the time. Your confidence and Faith in a Higher Power and His ability to help you be happy and stay happy, irrespective of your circumstance today or tomorrow will help create and maintain an abiding form of happiness and self fulfillment.

CHAPTER 12

DESIRE AND HAPPINESS

.

THE NATURE OF DESIRE

Desire plays a crucial role in one's ability to be happy today and to stay happy tomorrow. Desire really is a two-edged sword. It has an ability to motivate one to be excited in the promise of its fulfillment. However, the other side of this sword is its ability to create extreme misery and frustration if it (desire) is not fulfilled.

Let us turn to the nature of Desire. Desire functions as an emotional response. The nature of Desire is its ability to trigger an emotional visualization of a dream. Desire involves getting something of value to the individual. Visualization of achievement of this valuable goal results in an emotional reaction, which on several occasions is quite spontaneous. The process of desire fruition results in release of unknown but vital amounts of energy, which result in action and motivation towards a certain, object or result.

Since our childhood we have utilized desire to get things we want and things we feel we need.

This powerful energy in the form of Desire binds us to the things we need and want and moves us towards fulfillment of a goal or objective, which ultimately results in fulfillment of our desire.

We are constantly acting in the external environment, seeking to achieve the fulfillment of numerous desires. Some desires work innately and seem to express themselves naturally or subconsciously.

Other desires seem to be influenced by social, family or environmental influences.

As long as most of our desires are being fulfilled or in the process of being fulfilled, an individual stays happy and ecstatic. However, if a desire is blocked from being fulfilled or has a difficulty of being fulfilled in the future, there appears to be an emotional backlash to this thwarted desire.

HOW DESIRE GETS IN THE WAY

When a desire does not get fulfilled, one experiences and expresses several levels of negative energy ranging from mild to extreme anger to depression and hopelessness to suicidal tendencies, as an extreme case.

Desire gets in the way of true happiness if an individual measures happiness as a result of desire fulfillment only and defines unhappiness as non-fulfillment of his desires.

The really true and wise person sees no connection between desire and happiness.

Very simply put, there are certain basic needs we all have, like owning a house, driving a car, having a happy home and enjoying the company of good friends whilst living in a free and democratic state. Desire is vital in achieving these minimum goals.

Once an individual gets beyond this fulfillment level of basic material needs, additional desires represent marginal value as far as personal happiness is concerned.

The great mistake we make as human beings is that we allow desire to control all our thoughts, feelings and actions. Blocked desires or unfulfilled desires immediately and instantaneously create a negative energy flow. This energy block can be very harmful if not understood properly.

Desire is the motivational energy which gets you from point A to point B in the fulfillment of your needs and wants----however, there comes a point in one's life, where through awareness, one needs to disregard and disassociate with the passion associated with future desire.

If one has the capacity to disassociate from the constant and incessant energy demands of desire----then one creates the time, space and opportunity to use this conserved energy to focus on living happily from moment to moment.

The positive energy released now has the uncanny ability to allow one to live Life happily and fully from moment to moment.

Where one has to draw this line is very important. This is a personal decision, which every one must make on their own.

When one feels that desire is getting in the way and creating more problems than opportunities, then one has to simply suspend the functions of desire and fall back on your value system to help you to discover a more authentic way of Living Life.

We will cover the area of personal value system later and show how and why this is critical in your quest for happiness now and in the future.

AND HOW DESIRE CAN BE YOUR BEST FRIEND

Desire is not a bad thing. Its application in your life can be bad at some points. Desire can move mountains and through effective visualization can be the wellspring for great human progress and achievement.

However, endless entertainment of desire can cause a very negative flow of energy. For several human beings, their entire Life is comprised of a never-ending stream of actions whose only purpose is desire fulfillment.

All of life energy gets used and utilized in entertaining and fulfilling a vast number of desires.

And Life becomes a never-ending battle of getting more and more desires fulfilled. This is where a line must be drawn. Use desire to move forward in your   External Life. However, control desire to create the space you need to allow your Life to be fulfilled in the present.

Desire is only a tool for personal Happiness---it is not the be all and end all of Life's method and purpose.

If one can find and use this subtle difference to one's advantage, then Desire can be your best friend and help you move mountains, while at the same point allow you non-disturbance of your deeper sense of Happiness.

An excess over-dependence on Desire to fulfill all of your Life results can be extremely dangerous and cause a lot of negative side reactions.

The choice is yours---- either use Desire as your best friend and get great Life results or be totally dependent on desire and get marginal or inferior life results accompanied with very little happiness.

CHAPTER 13

YOUR HOUSE OF CARDS AND HOW IT CAN COLLAPSE OVERNIGHT

At times, we tend to take progress for granted. Sometimes when good things happen to us, we feel Life will continue to shower us with blessings and good results in the future, too. Unknown to us is the invisible Hand of Nature with its own set of priorities for us.

And sometimes, quite suddenly and unexpectedly, things change dramatically in our Lives. We could suddenly fall flat on the floor and wonder how we got there in the first place. Only yesterday we were on Cloud 9 and everything was so beautiful.

In context of your quest for a truly happy Life, how do you make sense of this sudden "nonsense" in your Life? How do you explain your going from being #1 to hitting the ground as a big zero?

True happiness is found in disassociating yourself from any and all Life results, whether such results are good, fair or poor. Your Life Result is not necessarily a reflection of your intelligence and effort. Life results have random movements and sometimes you can find yourself on the wrong side of a Life Result.

How you face any life threatening or temporary failing can make a difference between a truly happy life and a Life which is frustrated and stressed out, accompanied with a feeling of being dependent on an outside result (for your happiness).

It is so important to have a strong foundation and value system, which will help you face and go beyond any temporary failing.

However, the understanding must be that Life will always throw out unexpected results in random sequence. The results never reflect your value as a Human Being, nor are these negative results a reflection of your future. Your Life is beautiful and separated from these results, whether such results are good or bad.

Your Life is promised to be bountiful and happy and temporary failings will always pass, if you have the proper attitude towards them.

Focus, reinforcement and practice of your Life Value System will go a long way to helping you stay happy all the time.

CHAPTER 14

BUILDING STRENGTH UNDER YOUR HOUSE OF CARDS---- INTANGIBLE VALUES REQUIRED

If one realizes that Life has the capacity and ability to throw off negative results, then one sees the necessity of adequate mental, emotional and spiritual preparation. Such preparation assures one that the focus is kept on the Game of Life with respect to one's Vision and that one can continue on this Journey of

Life with maximum joy and Happiness, being uninfluenced by any temporary negative external result.

Nothing is more important in assuring this Happiness than your value and foundation system. What is the necessary foundation of values required?

Your foundation of core values delineated below will go a long way in your search for true Happiness in your Life. You may choose to add additional points to your own special and unique value system.

FOUNDATION OF CORE VALUES

1. We are all God-like creatures.

2. We derive our Power and Capacity from a Force much stronger than us.

3. Our challenge in Life is to meditate and bring the good Nature of this Force into our day-to-day existence.

4. All value, all happiness and harmony emanates from this Ever Energizing and Omnipotent Force.

174

5. Our responsibility and challenge in Life is to attract the happiness and high energy residing in this All-pervading force into our daily Lives.

6. While living our Life, we must be guided by the following principles representing Truth, Equality and Justice. (a) We must represent ourselves truthfully in all our commercial activities. (b) We must realize that all human beings are made Equal in God's eyes and this realization must bring great

175

humility in all our contacts and relationships with others. (c) We must be fair and just in all our dealings with others. (d) We must strive to give more to others than we receive as a reward or compensation for our activities connected to providing service to others.

7. We must have an open and positive mind to all experiences in our world.

8. We must maintain a positive attitude at all times.

9. We must believe that only we, individually can affect our Life attitudes--- therefore if you maintain a positive attitude and expectation for your life, success and happiness will ultimately be yours.

10. No adversity is bigger than Life or your Happiness.

11. Every adversity exists to teach you something new. It is your challenge to find out what hidden message Life is sending out to you to become a better, more integrated human being.

12. You refuse to feel negative in any thought, feeling or action.

13. You have no room for melancholy or negativism or depression in your Life. You and only you control the quality of your emotions. No external experiences however negative will affect your positive attitude and Happiness today.

14. You will meditate through awareness of all things happening outside you and inside you.

15. You will work consciously to improve the quality of your external and inner environment, through positive goal setting, visualization and prayer.

16. No negative external Life result will compel you to shy away from your goals and ideals to live a totally happy and self-actualized Life.

17. You will not strive for immediate perfection or for instant fulfillment or happiness. Rather, you will wait for happiness to enter your Life.

Your positive thoughts, feelings and actions will, in time, bring happiness automatically to your Life.

18. You will always be happy. Your happiness is unconditional and a God given right. Your happiness is not conditional on any external Life results or on any situation involving fulfillment or non-fulfillment of your desires. You will use Prayer as a way of finding out how to solve problems in your Life and in your dream of becoming a better human being.

Through creation and application of intangible values outlined above, you will be able to sustain a life of External and Inner success and be able to keep your Happiness intact in any and every situation of your Life.

CHAPTER 15

LOVE, COMPASSION AND SPIRITUALITY

Finding and maintaining Love marks one of the most important turning points in one's Life. Without Love and Happiness, Life has no meaning at all. The quality of Love is most important. Love is not conditional nor is it restricted to something or some person who may be the object of your affection. Love is truly impersonal,

182

Love towards an unknown stranger, love towards the Universe, love and care of all living things and a reverence for Life and Nature form critical components of your foundation of values.

Love needs to be constantly present in all relationships to make Life meaningful and to assure you a High Level of Peace and Happiness. Compassion on the other hand is a special reverence to everything around you. Compassion is not pity but a symbolization of Love at an extremely high level.

Spirituality is the highest aspect of the search for self-actualization. Spirituality consists of man's search for meaning and significance in relationship to his Life.

In this process, one goes deep inside oneself to understand the makeup and motivation of one's personality. One delves deep within to find out the nature of needs and wants and searches for a meaning, which may be beyond the capacity of the Mind. Meditation and awareness become critical parts of the spirituality process, which help one live Life with Simplicity, Grace and Happiness.

The challenge of Life calls for the exercise of Love, Compassion and Spirituality in the quest for true Happiness and Peace within you.

CHAPTER 16

THE CASE FOR SPIRITUALISM

When one looks at Life, there are numerous things, which cannot be explained easily. Why were we born in a particular part of the world? Why were we born in a particular family? Why did we have no choice in our acquisition of our early family values through our parents? Why did certain environmental and genetic factors influence the way we grew up? How and why has Life treated us of late?

Why are the Life results we have had so good or so bad, in spite of our best efforts?

This and numerous other questions cannot be easily answered. As we go about our Life, it is important to understand and accept that there are Forces influencing and affecting us daily. It is our challenge to be in touch with these Forces and make them work in our favor and not against us.

Spiritualism offers a way of connecting with our innermost selves---in the process it gives us a way of understanding ourselves in relationship with our environment, in relationship with other people and in relationship with ideas and material possessions.

Spiritualism offers the only hope to maintain our happiness in the future.

Spiritualism represents the process of self-realization. Only after we understand ourselves completely can we hope to find a way of living positively and harmoniously in our External and Inner world.

Spiritualism forms the missing key to making our Life truly happy and harmonious in every way. Spiritualism also frees one from the conditionality of Life. Our happiness becomes truly unconditional and has nothing to do with how rich or how fulfilled goal wise we may be.

Spiritualism is the missing link to our Happiness. If we can cultivate and understand it through intensive awareness and self-study we have a hope of rising beyond our mundane life.

Now we really have a Hope of making our Life truly beautiful and graceful.

The case for spiritualism is clear and strong----how come we have so few takers of this way of Existence?

CHAPTER 17

A PARTICULAR MESSAGE FOR NON-ACHIEVERS AND DEPRESSED SOULS---ITS NOT THE END OF THE WORLD

The world is filled with a great proportion of non-achievers. Let me define what I mean by a non-achiever. There are two levels of evaluation of a non-achiever.

One, there is the all mighty presence of the social and cultural background, influencing and controlling the definition of what a successful achiever is and a failing non-achiever is. This dictates what achievement symbolizes and, in default, what non-achievement is.

The other level of evaluation is that applied by an individual, based on his own values and perceptions on either progress or lack of progress in his Life.

The individual may borrow the societal and cultural definition of achievement and if he does not measure up to that, brand himself a non-achiever. Or he may have an inherently unique and personal definition of the word, "achievement." He might, for example, measure himself against his own definition of achievement, which could involve his ability to get most of the things he wants and desires.

If he cannot consistently reach his goals and dreams in a satisfactory manner, depression may set in and he may consider himself a non-achiever.

Please note that an individual is constantly defining himself as an achiever or non-achiever. He does this either consciously or sub-consciously.

The definition and subsequent behavior of a non-achiever is subtle and sometimes difficult to understand. He may walk tall, appearing to be proud and independent but deep down, a certain sense of loneliness lurks. There is quite clearly a lack of self-confidence.

Along with this is the inability of the person to make decisions--- this is sometimes followed by degrees of indecisiveness in his deeper. Personal relationships. Somehow, such an individual considers himself a good-for-nothing and is afraid sub-consciously from entering into any kind of permanent personal relationship.

A very clear impact emotionally in such non-achievers is a paucity of personal Happiness. And this is almost always accompanied by sporadic bouts of depression.

Such a non-achiever must realize that it is not the end of the world if he has not been able to consistently achieve his goals and dreams. Sometimes the goals and dreams may be unrealistic and a mere revision/modification of some of these goals may help restore his confidence and happiness.

Sometimes his pre-set goals and dreams may exceed his capacity and grasp----in this case, it would be wise to scale down his goals and expectations----in this process he may re-gain his confidence as he achieves slightly reduced goals.

With increased confidence as a result of winning, he may restore his balance and move from a state of non-achievement to a condition of achievement, success and relative satisfaction. The wisest non-achievers accept their results as is. They simply try to disassociate from the depression and lack of self-confidence resulting from non-achievement of a current goal.

By refusing to fail as a result of this conscious disassociation with current results, they gather all the lost and dissipated energy and re-channel this energy in their chosen endeavor.

They realize that in time, they will hit their goals---the real challenge is to gather and focus all their energy in their chosen field of endeavor and apply positive thinking and visualization to get what they want.

Non-achievers, who realize they are wasting their Life with unwanted fears and depression, quickly learn to accept themselves in whatever position they are in now and quickly re-align their energy to move in the direction of their dreams.

Another approach, which might help, is the one, which looks at the relevance of the external results of non-achievers. If these individuals view these results as just a temporary external phenomenon and not as the end of their world, they will soon have the courage and energy to tackle their goals and circumstances more effectively.

Everything is in the attitude----if you believe you can create miracles in your Life, then you will.

If you believe that with time and enthusiasm you can transform your life from a non-achiever to an achiever that is fine. However, if you cannot transform your life or will not put the effort to do so, then that is fine too.

Merely accept the quality of your results and stay happy at whatever point you are at now. Happiness is not always the achievement of a predetermined goal. Sometimes happiness involves accepting your situation and your weaknesses and allowing yourself to flow with your Life, wherever it takes you.

A supreme level of awareness is required to absolutely prevent any negative energy or depression from slowing you down in your pursuit of your goals and dreams.

Do not forget, happiness is inside and not outside you. If the outside cannot give you what you want, then do not give the outside much emphasis.

Try to develop your inner spiritual values. Try to refine and expand your inner psychological value system.

Keep happy and positive and enthusiastic. Apply the maximum quantum of energy in your tasks, whatever this task may be.

Non-achievement in any sense is not the end of the world. It is a one- time or two- time phenomenon, which is happening outside you. Non-achievement does not dictate who you are and what you stand for. It is merely a lesson for you to grow and become a better person now and in the future.

CHAPTER 18

YOU HAVE EVERYTHING YOU NEED

We sometimes forget that we have the capacity and energy to realize all of our dreams. We fail to recognize that we are responsible for all the energy blocks, which come in the way of achievement of one's dreams and goals. So how does one go about tapping into this mysterious but powerful source of Energy residing within?

Meditation is undoubtedly the most effective channel to help one direct one's energy flow inward.

Meditation, when done properly, creates an awareness of one's weaknesses and emotional flaws. If one properly observes oneself one can see where one's energy blocks are. One can notice that through anger,anxiety, lack of self-confidence or emotional distraction, one cheats oneself energy-wise. If energy is not applied fully and completely at one point then it is diffused. Diffused energy always creates inferior Life results.

Most individuals feel that they cannot quickly improve their energy concentration and flow in a specific task. The results therefore continue to be mediocre with no increase in task productivity.

Once you find your energy sources and centers, then through awareness, positive thinking, enthusiasm and faith, you can move your energy in a direction, which helps you fulfill your tasks and goals easily.

Let us now talk about specific meditation techniques you can use to achieve positive results in your Life.

MEDITATION TECHNIQUE I

Sit in a quiet place uninterrupted by people or music. Find a quiet room in your house or in your office. This technique is best used twice a day. First, as soon as you wake up and wash your face you can start your day this way.

Imagine yourself being a passenger in an express train going from one city to another. Imagine this journey to last fifteen minutes (the recommended time for your initial meditation class).

Imagine yourself looking out of the train window, observing things happening outside you.

Let us imagine your train going through beautiful farmland and you see farmers harvesting their fields. You watch the farmers as a witness. You are really not involved with these farmers since you do not know them personally. However, your attention is still on their work and activity.

Very soon, your train passes through these farm fields and heads up a small mountain.

You again look at the beautiful mountain with all the lush vegetation.

Your attention suddenly halts at a mountain goat trying to climb this mountain.

Again, the mountain and the mountain goat are outside you. You have no direct connection with them. However you silently watch them as a witness. Your attention is detached but alive and aware in every way.

Meditation involves witnessing everything inside and outside you. Now close your eyes and be quiet. Immediately, across the screen of your mind will flash numerous thoughts and feelings.

Instead of associating intimately with these thoughts and feelings, imagine these thoughts and feelings to be like the farmers pasturing their land and the mountain and mountain goat in the train episode earlier. Just watch and witness all these thoughts and feelings with no judgment. Do this for about fifteen minutes. You can set an alarm to time yourself in this process.

MEDITATION TECHNIQUE 2

Before you sleep in the night, go through the same exercise at technique 1. In addition after you finish fifteen minutes of this process, start thinking of all the activities you engaged in during the entire day. Start looking at each activity from the time you woke up to the time you prepare to sleep in the night. Could you have done anything better or differently this day?

This additional exercise allows your mind to rest during your sleep session. It also allows your Mind to reconstitute itself before you enter deep sleep and assures you better sleep in the night.

The objective of these two meditation techniques is to open up some "special inner centers". Through meditation one opens up one's Self-awareness. Once your meditation becomes intensive, you are more aware of all your feelings and thoughts naturally.

By negating feelings of lack of self-confidence and depression, you create an avenue for positivism to come into your life.

Just by negating all anger and anxiety, you can create the space and energy necessary for you to move in the direction of your dreams and goals. Just as you cannot be positive and negative at the same time, it is extremely hard for you to be confident and depressed at the same time. If you can actively manage your depression through self-awareness, then by default you have invited confidence in your life.

By the same token when you negate anger and anxiety you create the circumstance and opportunity for love and happiness to come right into your Life----you create a high-energy inner zone. You can then use this high-energy zone to fulfill your dreams and goals (and to keep you happy always).

The challenge before a human being is to find this energy, gather it and re-direct it to stay happy and focused in the fulfillment of his dreams and goals.

Happiness is promised to us-----but to earn this promise, we need to be eternally self-vigilant and throw out anger, anxiety and depression by choosing not to entertain these feelings at any time in our life.

Happiness is our Destiny---we must believe in this Destiny and put our effort and awareness in living this Life with great Peace and Love.

CHAPTER 19

STRESS MANAGEMENT AND RELATIONSHIP BUILDING

Stress is one of the greatest causes of pain in our Life today. To be happy with where you are today, you must have a reasonable handle on this situation called Stress. And, fortified with ideas, techniques and methods, you must attempt to conquer Stress while maintaining your Happiness today and building and reinforcing the seeds of happiness and success tomorrow.

Stress usually marks a perceived gap between what you have and what you want. Let me explain.

You have a vision of how you would like your Life to be. You look at your Life today and see that many things you have wanted in your Life have either not materialized or do not have any hope of materializing in the very near future. You see a gap in several relationships. This perceived gap is then amplified by your emotions and intellect resulting in a reaction.

Depending on your mental and nervous constitution and on your ability to withstand pain, this reaction can either be moderate, intense or muted. Once this reaction sets in, it could take a toll on you physically. This reaction could find some vulnerable physical organ and direct its effect there. If you have a weak heart or weak eyes, it attacks such organs. Physical maladies ensue and have the potential of creating further problems.

Stress management starts with first
accepting that there will be some
gaps in your Life.

Also, it starts with knowing that you
cannot control the immediate reaction
to a stressor (a stressor is the
stimulus or situation, which is
responsible for triggering a stress
reaction). However, it allows you to
give yourself the ability to negate the
reaction effect by boldly refusing to
accept defeat or distress by this
natural reaction amplification. This is
where your value system is so
important in not allowing further
amplification of this reaction.

Awareness is one of the most effective, long-term reliable weapons, which can be immediately employed to manage stress.

If you are not aware of your reaction to a stressor, then how can you modify its impact on your physical and emotional constitution? It is impossible if you are not eternally aware.

Life is a constant, shifting, churning process of Energy. As external circumstances change, so do your reactions to these changes.

Therefore the price for effective stress management is eternal awareness and a real understanding of the causes of stress in your Life.

Awareness is the first step. Now, how do you go about changing the immediate reaction to a stressor?

By merely superimposing your value system on the screen of your mind. This is pretty simple.

Imagine you wanting to have a certain personal relationship at a certain point of time. You do not have it at this moment. On the screen of our mind is a thought flash, which says, " I am not feeling good now.

I am really unhappy that I have not been able to attract a certain type/quality of relationship in my Life now." This perception is verbalized here----it may be in fact an emotional perception translating to what the verbal definition is.

At this point, most individuals try to block this perception or escape it through some distraction (like wine, women and song). One must at this point, hold on to this image of emptiness of a perceived gap. Do not validate it or escape from it. Just stay with it. This is extremely difficult to do in the beginning.

But if you stay with it, you will be able to move out of this perceptive image and change it. Now, on the flashing screen of your Mind, superimpose a new image of Love, confidence and happiness. This image is a happy, unconditional image, which brings brightness and positivism to your Life. Now again superimpose some of the things you want in our Life. Superimpose it on the initial perception. If you do this often enough, you will find that the negative emotional perception has disappeared and it has been replaced by a happy perception.

At the least, there will be an absence of the negative perception. Once the negative perception has disappeared, you will have additional energy and space to achieve your dreams and goals.

Now let us look at the connection between stress and relationships.

Life is nothing but a complex web of relationships. The quality and intensity of such relationships vary in every person's Life. To improve your Life, you need to increase the intensity of valuable relationships,in addition to improving the quality and depth of all existing relationships.

Sometimes you may have to replace certain relationships to enhance the quality of your Life. Stress never exists in a vacuum. Stress always exists in relationship to an idea, thing, person or possession.

Stress always indicates a lack of quality in a certain relationship.

Think about this seriously. If you close your eyes and feel a disturbance somewhere in your psyche---can you study the source of this disturbance? Usually, this disturbance is a gap between what you want and what you have today.

For example, you may seek a passionate loving experience with your mate----you and she have had a bitter fight today and all the Love has gone out the window. You feel hurt, distressed and lost. You wanted intimacy and what you got at this moment was anger and apathy.

This is where the stress starts. Your mate has become the negative stressor. The stress has been caused by the gap in the relationship at this moment. You have an expectation of love at this moment and instead you've got pain.

225

In order to remove this stress you either need to understand your mate better or in an extreme case, leave this mate and find someone more suitable.

Stress acts as an inhibitor to Love and Happiness. So, the more stress you eliminate, the happier you are, period.

To eliminate Stress, you need to study each and every Life relationship you have now.

You then need to analyze the quality, depth and intensity of each Life relationship and then determine where the Stress is coming from.

226

A good way of understanding and applying these Rules to Relationships is to prioritize every relationship in your Life now.

Let us suppose these are the levels of relationships you have now:

LEVEL 1(MOST IMPORTANT)
Relationships with life partner, children and family and friends.

LEVEL 2 (VERY IMPORTANT)
Relationships with: money, possessions, and other material things.

LEVEL 3 (IMPORTANT)

Relationships with employer, boss and co-workers.

LEVEL 4 (LESS IMPORTANT)

Relationships with church, religious advisors.

LEVEL 5 (NOT VERY IMPORTANT)

Relationships with your immediate neighbors,

Relationships with your body through health.

LEVEL 6

(UNIMPORTANT)

Relationships with certain ideas and certain possessions.

You need to go through every relationship with a fine tooth and comb. At the end of analysis of each relationship you must ask yourself the following questions:

1. Am I satisfied with the quality and depth of this relationship?
2. Am I satisfied with the intensity of this relationship?

3. Am I satisfied with the priority I have given to this relationship in my Life?
4. Is it important to elevate in priority or de-elevate the importance of this relationship?
5. Is there anything I can do to improve this relationship by making any changes in it?
6. Should I drop this relationship completely or replace it with something, which will improve the quality of my Happiness in my Life?

7. Is this relationship in any way creating stress in my Life? And if so where are the gaps in this relationship----gaps between my expectations and the reality of this relationship?

8. What else can I learn through this relationship?

9. What can I do through this relationship to increase my Level of Happiness in this Life? Can I accept the current state of this relationship or do I need to understand it better to live a Life of unconditional Happiness?

You can improve the quality of your Life through active stress management---leading to stress reduction. An active analysis and understanding of the existing relationships in your Life will result in a more happier and beautiful life for you.

CHAPTER 20

BRINGING IT ALL TOGETHER

Now I would like to recap all the prominent ideas in this book.

We started our journey together by proposing a concept that we, as human beings, had the capacity to be happy, at whatever station in Life we were in now. We explored the idea that happiness, to be effective and permanent, had to be unconditional in nature.

The entire book pursued the idea of building a framework in which peace, harmony and happiness could prevail in our Life.

One of the first ideas propounded was that of an individual becoming consciously aware that happiness could be won on a moment-to-moment basis-----this was possible if one did not allow thought comparisons and expectations to cloud our vision of happiness. As soon as we started comparing our past with our imagined future, there would be the creation of mental and emotional gaps, which would

234

exacerbate the differences between reality today and our imagined future. This most definitely would attract anxiety and unhappiness---the exact opposite of what we needed and deserved from our Life.

The mission statement of this book challenged you to go beyond your comfort zone and work at creating a totally harmonious and peaceful life. Such a life was possible with the right attitude and meditation.

We started the first part of he book by talking about your personal Road Ahead.

We took some time to explore some of the thoughts and feelings, which one would experience when one looked at one's personal Road Ahead.

We then took an inventory of your Life by looking at exactly where you were today in relationship to where you wanted to go tomorrow and with respect to how you needed to feel to be unconditionally happy today.

Our next part of the journey looked at three interesting and somewhat contradictory concepts:

Firstly, where we wanted to go to tomorrow (our heart),

Secondly, where we thought we should go tomorrow (our mind and intellectual machinations) &

Thirdly, where we felt we ought to be tomorrow (societal and environmental demands on where we should be).

We then looked at how one needed to resolve these three conflicts to build a firm and strong footing for unconditional happiness.

We then looked at your personal environment and did a preview of the many obstacles you may have to face in the achievement of your dreams and goals.

We then proceeded to look at healthy ways of overcoming your obstacles in your quest for happiness and peace today.

Now we introduced the concept of success. Success, we discovered was a highly rated and misunderstood word.

We went into one, overriding definition of success and tried to make sense of your success as it related to your happiness and harmony in the world around you.

We then discussed the illusion of a destination as a common end or resting point of our dreams and goals.

We looked at the fact that Success and Life were both a process of living and not a goal per se.

We then looked at the differences between external (material) success and inner success and how important it was to combine them.

We then looked at the conflict process faced by us in our struggle to arrive inwardly and suggested newer and better ways of arriving at Success and Happiness, as compared to just struggling inwardly.

We then focused our attention on the nature of Desire and how Desire could be either a curse or blessing (in our pursuit of happiness and success).

Life in its intrinsic mystery and uncertainty had an uncanny ability to create change. What appeared to be stable and solid on the external front yesterday could suddenly collapse like a pack of cards today.

It seemed so important to have a strong value foundation to withstand any unforeseen changes in your Life. Examples incorporating a strong value system were next discussed.

Love, compassion and spirituality as important elements of one's Life were now discussed. The relationship of these three major attributes (love, compassion and spirituality) toward one's success and happiness were discussed.

Special mention was made of the value afforded to an individual embracing spirituality (as an essential component of a long-term foundation for success and happiness).

Special consideration was given in this book to individuals who considered themselves as depressed souls.

Such individuals considered themselves as non-achievers and had lost the will and courage to keep fighting to find a beautiful path into their future.

An idea was proposed here to help such individuals look at their Life differently and to work towards a foundation of success and happiness. We then discussed how important it was to focus your energy in your task at hand to get Life results compatible with your dreams, desires and needs.

Two specific meditation techniques were proposed to assist the reader harness his energy in the direction of his dreams and goals.

We then looked at how important it was to reduce the quantum of stress in our lives and how the challenge of Life boiled down to optimizing all our personal relationships.

Great care was taken to show an individual how to analyze and understand the various relationships in his life----how to prioritize these relationships and how to optimize them for good health, wealth, prosperity & unconditional happiness.

243

The ultimate goal was to improve the quality and intensity of chosen relationships leading to a happy and peaceful life for the reader.

A FEW PARTING WORDS FROM THE AUTHOR

REBUILDING YOUR LIFE FOUNDATION

One may find that one's value foundation is not strong enough to weather Life's storms. Or one may find that one's value foundation is not well crystallized and developed.

244

This may prevent one from applying enough energy to withstanding any negative effects of circumstance.

If one's life foundation is not well developed, then one needs to re-build this life foundation.

Try to build a code of conduct and strong values embracing your thoughts to Life and use this conduct and value system to keep your focus on happiness today and happiness tomorrow. Do remember the only way to be happy is to unconditionally accept your situation today.

Try to improve your situation tomorrow but do not base your happiness on achieving the improvement tomorrow. It is all in the attitude and state of mind.

Through calmness and acceptance, you have a greater Power to change things today than through anxiety, competition and disharmony.

Happiness is only granted to those who work at their unconditional acceptance of today's state and tomorrow's results, whatever these results may be.

REPERCEIVING AND RESTRENGTHENING EVERY RELATIONSHIP AND ASPECT OF YOUR LIFE

Do study the chapter on stress management and relationship building. If you find you have wrongly prioritized any of your relationships, then this perception should allow you to build new relationships or reprioritize existing ones to create more quality in your Life. One needs to work hard at re-strengthening all relationships in one's life to improve the quality of one's happiness.

BUILDING AND COMBINING SPIRITUAL VALUES WITH MATERIAL SUCCESS

It is quite easy to get caught up in the external material life. One becomes so involved with external events, that sometimes one sub-consciously accepts this as the be all and end all of one's Life.

One simply fails to take heed of all the inner functioning's of one's mind, heart and soul. Building and nurturing spiritual values is more important than just having fun on the outside.

248

There is absolutely nothing wrong with having fun----however external pleasure must be balanced with inner strength and values. This combination results in tranquility from both within and without and works wonders in your quest for success and happiness. Success and happiness are both synonymous in Life terms.

You cannot be successful and unhappy, nor is it possible to be happy and unsuccessful.

These two states of success and happiness are shadows of each other and where one is, the other is right behind. Happiness will assure you success at every level of existence.

CHAPTER 21

SUMMARY

This thesis talks about the simple and beautiful Life ahead of you. It tries to show you that you have everything here and now to be Happy. It also throws out a challenge to you to discover and enjoy your Life in the here and now.

Beauty, Happiness and Love are our natural birthrights.

We need to develop the capacity to reach this Higher Level of Consciousness. The World is crying for positive change, leading to unconditional happiness. Existence is crying. All of Nature and Life are crying and urging Mankind to make necessary and fundamental changes to align with the Greater Divine Force. You, as a human being, have this marvelous and natural capacity to discover a new dimension in your Life.

You and you alone are responsible for this effort and process of bringing Happiness back to your Life.

His gift of unconditional and constant happiness is achievable in your present Lifetime.

A heightened level of Awareness, a serious meditation stance, an active Loving Life, an optimization of all your relationships and a massive reduction in stress will all contribute to a Life truly happy and graceful.

In this way, you would have justified your Existence.

You have this precious moment now. Make the best use of it. Enjoy it unconditionally. Make Life the most beautiful gift you can relish.

I truly wish you the best of success in your quest to live Life happily and to the fullest extent of your natural capacities and God given talent.

CHAPTER 22

CONCLUSION & BOOK SYNOPSIS

Life is a beautiful and mysterious experience. Through our lifetime we consciously and sub-consciously attempt to improve the quality and content of our experiences and relationships. Life is nothing but a series of relationships----if you choose to improve your life, you need to necessarily improve the quality and intensity of your relationships.

We all try to live a better Life-----
however, deep down, hidden within
us is the true barometer of how we
feel about our environment and
ourselves.

If we feel good about our Life,   we
re-create the capacity to live a better
tomorrow. On the other hand, if we feel
depressed and hopeless about our
future prospects, then this negative
energy influences our life through poor
results tomorrow.

Being happy today and trusting the
universe to continue your happiness
tomorrow is the gist of this publication.

You really possess everything today to be happy.

You have it all now.....your life is truly yours to discover and enjoy.

As you look at your personal road ahead, you must be aware of all the different directions your mind and heart operate in. There is obviously conflict between what you feel you want (emotional motivation), what you think you need (intellectual motivation) and what you ought to do with your Life (societal and peer group motivation). Sorting out this chaos and bringing order in your life by understanding and adjusting harmoniously these three levels of influence is paramount.

Understanding your environmental influences and learning to rise above them is important in being happy and staying happy. Desire plays an important role in your ability to attract and maintain happiness in your life. Both outer and inner success need to work hand-in-hand to provide optimum happiness in your Life.

Love and happiness are the only reasons for Life and the only motivating factors for success.

This book attempts to create an understanding of several mental, emotional, intellectual and spiritual forces affecting your life today.

This book tries to show you that peace, happiness and harmony are very close to you.

A strong value system, an open heart and mind, a positive attitude and a kindness to all human beings are the foundation for a Life filled with grace, harmony and goodness.

You have it all now----your Life is urging to be discovered and enjoyed. Success is your birthright and destiny. Success is really being happy and accepting of whatever position you face in your life today. Success is not reaching anywhere.

Success is being happy in your life position today. When accompanied by an unconditional acceptance of whatever results Existence brings your way tomorrow, you have the perfect recipe for everlasting happiness. Life is a special gift from the Almighty-----we must live fully in this moment. This moment is all that is promised to us. The author's wish and prayer is to serve as a guide in the process of allowing every reader of this book, the opportunity to discover and enjoy their Life in their own unique and special way.

Live Life passionately, energetically and completely with no fear or worry of tomorrow. Only complete unconditional acceptance of your situation now and an unwavering trust in the Almighty's ability to guarantee you happiness tomorrow can result in a complete, satisfying and fulfilled Life. You have Happiness near to you-----use your God-given power to live Life uniquely and happily in every relationship.

APPENDIX 1

BARRIERS TO PERSONAL HAPPINESS

COMMUNICATION AS A MEANS OF CONFLICT RESOLUTION

So many times in Life, there are situations, which involve resolution of conflicts. A conflict only arises inside a relationship. A conflict represents a gap between your expectation and reality in a relationship at a certain point of time.

Gaps occur in the best of relationships through the passage of time.

Let us look at some potential conflict situations:

1. Conflicts in personal relationships, with a loved one, a friend or a family member.
2. Conflict with your employer or business partner.
3. Conflicts with your natural environment.
4. Conflicts involving money relationships.

5. Conflicts involving poor health-
    ---this reflects a poor
    relationship with your body.

A conflict becomes a cause for unhappiness. Resolution of a conflict can clear the way for happiness---it cannot guarantee it.

Life is a series of relationships and to increase one's personal happiness, one must try to improve the quality and intensity of your valued relationships. It is critical to look at all current and possible potential conflict situations in one's Life in order to clear the ground for happiness to set into your Life.

An important starting point is the realization that you are not the conflict----the conflict exists outside you. Your misunderstanding of a situation or your being misunderstood may create and sustain a conflict. Whatever the source and cause of the conflict, it is important to analyze the conflict thoroughly and understand, in an unbiased fashion. the reasons for it. Are you creating the conflict out of unrealistic expectations?

Or is the other one in the relationship simply not responding to your needs and expectations? Sometimes, the only remedy may be to exit a relationship for your sanity and peace.

Conflicts create energy blocks and such blocks prevent the creation and sustenance of long-term happiness. It is so important to put all your conflicts on the table with intent to resolving most or all of them.

Absence of conflict is impossible as long as you live in the world and deal with other human beings-----but an intelligent understanding and analysis of such conflicts will go a long way in helping you to smoothen out your relationships and clear the way for happiness to set in.

An important start in this road to happiness is the acceptance that no one or nothing on the outside can give you happiness. If you feel empty inside and feel that another person can brighten your life up permanently, then you are setting yourself up for a major future emotional calamity.

One must first work at creating the energy and happiness spark within through meditation, awareness and introspection. Then, when one is happy and whole and complete may one look for someone to share the happiness with. An improper partner can create havoc in a relationship----- maybe, it is better to let go and be alone, even for a short period of time then to engage in a relationship just because one is bored or wants to escape from one's loneliness.

Love is truly impersonal. Love, in its greatest form, creates a total and unbounded appreciation of all the beautiful things around you----towards Nature, towards birds and animals, towards the beauty of this universe and to others in relationships with you. There is no exclusivity to Love. In fact, exclusivity destroys the Spirit and Beauty of Love.

Can you love your life partner without jealousy and possessiveness? Can you be happy when you are physically (far) away from your partner? Love is caring, sharing and being happy.

When exclusivity comes in, it destroys the fabric of Love. If you have this emotional vulnerability and dependence on someone else for Love, then you could be setting yourself up in a conflict situation. Understanding and acceptance of ones vulnerability and the starting of a capacity to love with detachment is the first step towards unbound happiness in your Life.

INDEX

A

B

C

272

D

E

E

F

G

H

I

J

K

L

M

N

O

P

P

R

S

S

T

U

V

W

AUTHOR INTRODUCTION

Mr. Raj D. Rajpal is a well-known and highly regarded personal and motivation trainer.

Through his young days in India and his middle years in North America, Raj has been an intensive student of People and Life.

He has constantly tried to go beyond the common platform of conventionality----he has endeavored to find value in things not normally considered important.

Raj has widely traveled the world. He has intense interest in personal self-development issues and has successfully explored and experimented with new ideas.

Raj has been a course and seminar leader in numerous business and personal development and motivation programs.

He was a certified instructor for the Larry Wilson Counselor Development Program and has personally assisted hundreds of individuals in their quest for more meaningful personal and business lives.

Raj believes he was put in this world to help others. This book is a condensation of several valuable Life lessons used successfully in personal training programs by Raj.

The author hopes you enjoy this book and use some of these principles to enhance the quality and intensity of relationships in your life.

Unconditional and complete Happiness today are natural birthrights of Man.

Why not claim them for your benefit and value today????

www.ingramcontent.com/pod-product-compliance
Lightning Source LLC
Chambersburg PA
CBHW060008100426
42740CB00010B/1439